Library of Shakespearean Biography and Criticism

I. PRIMARY REFERENCE WORKS ON SHAKESPEARE

II. CRITICISM AND INTERPRETATION

    A. Textual Treatises, Commentaries
    B. Treatment of Specal Subjects
    C. Dramatic and Literary Art in Shakespeare

III. SHAKESPEARE AND HIS TIME

    A. General Treatises. Biography
    B. The Age of Shakespeare
    C. Authorship

Series II, Part C

THE TREATMENT OF
SHAKESPEARE'S TEXT...

Library of Shakespearean Biography and Criticism

ANNUAL SHAKESPEARE LECTURE

THE TREATMENT OF SHAKESPEARE'S TEXT BY HIS EARLIER EDITORS, 1709-1768

By RONALD B. McKERROW

Fellow of the Academy

Read April 26, 1933

 BOOKS FOR LIBRARIES PRESS

FREEPORT, NEW YORK

First Published 1933
Reprinted 1970

STANDARD BOOK NUMBER·
8369-5265-0

LIBRARY OF CONGRESS CATALOG CARD NUMBER:
79-109656

PRINTED IN THE UNITED STATES OF AMERICA

THE TREATMENT OF SHAKESPEARE'S TEXT BY HIS EARLIER EDITORS, 1709–1768

By RONALD B. McKERROW

Fellow of the Academy

Read April 26, 1933

THE last few years have seen so much new work done on the text of Shakespeare, so much development in critical method, and so many fresh theories involving ever greater concentration on the minute study of the earliest forms in which his plays were printed, that there seems to have been of late a disposition to ignore, as something out of date and wholly superseded, the work done by the editors of the eighteenth century, and to forget the thanks which are due to them for their share in making Shakespeare accessible to the reading public.

It is perfectly true that in a sense their work, like that of all pioneers, has been superseded, and that almost any person of quite moderate attainments and experience could nowadays, working from the early editions and with the aids now available in the form of dictionaries, concordances, grammars, and the like, produce a text of Shakespeare which would be regarded by scholars as far superior to those of the eighteenth-century editors. So far as pure scholarship is concerned we might now, without more than such moral damage as a lack of decent gratitude can do one, forget them altogether and let them and their too numerous quarrels rest in peace. But in the matter of literature, scholarship is not everything. Besides and apàrt from the few who *study* the work of Shakespeare, there are thousands in all parts of the world who read him solely for pleasure. Such readers have, as a rule, no need for the kind of edition which appeals to the modern scholar. What *they* require is rather what the eighteenth-century editors aimed at producing, and did in fact produce, a text which is easy to read

1

and intelligible, without asperities either of grammar or of metre, and provided with all those helps in the way of stage directions, indications of locality, and the like which enable the lazy-minded to fathom the meaning without puzzlement and the lover of literature to savour the poetry without distraction. In spite of the work of the last 150 years, Shakespeare, as he is known in the literature, not only of our own country, but of the world, is still in the main the Shakespeare of Rowe, Pope, Theobald, Johnson, and the other eighteenth-century editors; and let me emphasize this afternoon that if it had not been for the less careful, I might almost say less respectful, treatment accorded to him by these earlier editors, he might never have reached the position in the world's esteem which has made the later scholarship seem worth while. Let us therefore pay a tribute of gratitude to them by attempting to study, so far as is possible in a brief hour, their attitude towards the text of Shakespeare and the work which they did upon it.

As you will remember, the folio volume of 1623, the 'First Folio', contained all the plays generally attributed to Shakespeare with the exception of *Pericles*. This volume was thrice reprinted—in 1632, the 'Second Folio'; in 1663, the 'Third Folio'; and in 1685, the 'Fourth Folio'. In the later issue of the Third Folio, and in the Fourth, were included seven additional plays attributed to Shakespeare, of which only one—*Pericles*—is generally printed in modern editions. Previous to 1623 nineteen plays (including *Pericles*) had been printed separately in quarto, and two or three were reprinted from one of the folios as quarto play-books later, but even at the end of the seventeenth century any one who wanted to read Shakespeare would for almost half his plays have had to turn to the inconveniently large two-columned folios. While he certainly *was* read in these folios, the more handy and readable editions produced in the eighteenth century undoubtedly had a great influence in widening the circle of Shakespeare's readers, while in its turn this greater popularity itself led to the multiplication of editions. As against the four folios of the seventeenth century from 1623 to 1685, we have in sixty years of the eighteenth century, from 1709 to 1768, editions by Rowe, Pope, Theobald, Hanmer, Warburton, Johnson, and Capell, and as most of these were reprinted at least once and some much more frequently, the total number of editions of Shakespeare's complete plays issued during the period amounts to twenty-five or thereabouts, indicating a very great increase in the attention paid to him by the reading public.

When we consider the editions of Shakespeare from the First Folio of 1623 to the edition of Pope a century later, we see very clearly the transition between the simple re-printing of an author regarded as contemporary and the 'editing' of one who has become out of date and somewhat difficult to understand, in order to present his text in as sound and intelligible a form as possible to a later public to whom he is no longer one of themselves.

The alterations made in the three later folios of 1632, 1663, and 1685 are for the most part merely the kind of alteration generally made in reprinting a contemporary or definitely *recent* author. They consist almost entirely of two kinds. Firstly, the correction of such misprints as happened to be noticed—we need say nothing about the introduction of new ones, for these were presumably unintentional—and, secondly, the normal modernizations in spelling and in various points of typographical practice which have at all times been usual in reprinting any book in which exact reproduction is not regarded as important.[1]

When, leaving the folios, we come, in 1709, to Rowe's edition, we find this normal modernization still continuing,[2] and indeed being carried somewhat further than in mere spelling, for Rowe frequently substituted modern *forms* of words for older ones, 'whilst' for 'whiles', 'been' for the old unemphatic form 'bin', 'an' for 'and' in the sense of 'if', 'he' for 'a' in such phrases as 'a rubs himself with civet', and so on; but with Rowe the more serious attention to the text as a whole begins to overshadow the mere local corrections of a kind that might be made by a compositor or proof-reader. What we understand by the 'editing' of Shakespeare has begun.

At the time when Rowe's edition was put in hand the position as regards the text of Shakespeare was as follows. There were on the one hand the four folio editions with their progressive modernizations, and on the other a number of quarto editions of single plays. These were of two kinds. There were, firstly, the original quartos printed before the date of the First Folio and for that reason representing an authority superior to, or at any rate different from, that of the folios. Some of these had continued to be reprinted up to Rowe's time as theatrical play-books. Thus there were *Hamlet* quartos of 1676, 1683, 1695, and 1703—indeed more than these, for three of these dates are found on two separate editions; one in each case being possibly a piracy. There were *Othellos* of 1655, 1681, 1687, 1695, and 1705, a *Merchant of Venice* of 1652, and a *Lear* of 1655. These all go back to the original quarto texts, though with a good deal of minor alteration. They are in fact, as stated on several of the title-pages, the play 'as it is now acted'. But besides these quartos there were also two or three which were merely reprints of the folio text. Thus there had been a *Taming of the Shrew* in 1631 and later there were quartos of *Julius Caesar* and *Macbeth*.

It seems to have been generally realized at the time that the printed texts of Shakespeare were bad, and also that there were differences between the folio and quarto versions. No serious attempt had, however, been made to work out the bibliography of the Shakespeare plays, and nothing better existed than the rough lists in Gerard Langbaine's *Account of the English Dramatic Poets*, 1691, and *Lives and Characters of the English Dramatic Poets* [1699]. Between them these mention quartos of nine plays, including *The Tempest*, *Macbeth*, and *Julius Caesar*, but the only dates given are late in the seventeenth century, with the odd exception of *Titus*

Andronicus which Langbaine dates as 1594, a date which was proved to be correct more than two hundred years later by the discovery of a copy in Sweden in 1904. How vague the knowledge on the subject was at the time and even later may be inferred from the fact that in 1722 Jacob Tonson, the publisher, was, in view of Pope's forthcoming edition, advertising for editions of *The Tempest, Macbeth, Julius Caesar, Timon of Athens, King John,* and *Henry VIII* printed before 1620.[3]

Nothing seems to be known as to the reason which moved Tonson to bring out a new edition of Shakespeare, but the matter is probably simple enough. In the early years of the eighteenth century there was, owing to the great amount of piratical printing and the uncertainty of the law, much agitation about copyright, and eventually an Act was passed for the regulation of this, more or less on present-day lines, coming into force in April 1710. Tonson, who was one of the largest London publishers, had some years earlier obtained the rights in the folio text of Shakespeare by purchase from the publishers of the Fourth Folio of 1685, and it seems not improbable that the edition of 1709 was undertaken, partly at any rate, with a view to calling atten-tion to his possession of these rights. Nicholas Rowe was probably as good a man as Tonson could have found to act as editor. Originally trained for the law, he had early devoted himself to theatrical affairs and for some ten years had been known as a writer for the stage. He had interested himself in Jacobean drama to the extent of producing an adaptation of Massinger's *Fatal Dowry*, and must altogether have seemed quite a suitable person to edit Shakespeare.

As Tonson appears to have paid Rowe only £36 10s. od. for his work on Shakespeare, which even considering the higher value of money at the time was not much, we may doubt if anything very elaborate was looked for. The edition was clearly intended as a popular one, for in spite of the forty-five engravings with which it was embellished, the price of the six volumes was only thirty shillings. Probably a considerable part of the remuneration paid to Rowe for his edition was for the Life of Shakespeare which he prefixed to it. This remained for many years the standard and indeed only 'Life' and was reprinted in almost all the editions of Shakespeare down to the 'Variorum' of 1821, and its admitted importance, in spite of the vast number of statements contained in it which have since been discredited, seems to some extent to have distracted attention from Rowe's treatment of the plays themselves.

Let us consider first what Rowe professed to do, and then what he actually did. His intentions are set forth in his Dedication to the Duke of Somerset, where having referred to the particular pleasure which he had heard the Duke express in 'that Greatness of Thought, those natural Images, those Passions finely touch'd, and that beautiful Expression which is everywhere to be met with in *Shakespeare*', he continues with a thoroughly eighteenth-century gesture:

And that he may still have the Honour to entertain Your Grace, I have taken some Care to redeem him from the Injuries of former Impressions.

He admits that it is impossible to restore the text to the exactness of the author's original manuscripts, as these are lost. He has, however, compared the several editions and, as well as he could, has given the true reading from thence, thus rendering very many places intelligible that were not so before. He continues:

In some of the Editions, especially the last, there were many Lines (and in *Hamlet* one whole Scene) left out altogether; these are now all supply'd.

This is a large claim, but we must see what he actually performed. By the 'last edition' he presumably meant the folio of 1685, and as regards *Hamlet*, the only play specifically mentioned, he carried out more or less what he claimed to do. He evidently collated one of the later quartos, that of 1676 or one still later, with the Fourth Folio, though perhaps rather hastily. As is well known, the

folio texts of *Hamlet* from the first onwards omit many lines
which are found in the second and later quartos. Of the
lines omitted—some 231—Rowe restored about 131, including 59 lines in Act IV, scene iv, which is presumably the
whole scene which he states to have been omitted in the
'last edition', though actually the folios give the first eight
lines of it. The other 100 lines omitted by the folios which
Rowe did not restore include a speech of 22 lines in
I. iv. 17–38 regarding the drunkenness of the Danes,

> This heavy-headed revel east and west
> Makes us traduced and taxed of other nations:

and 41 lines of Hamlet's talk with Osric in v. ii. 109–50.
These at least must, I think, be intentional omissions, though
some of the shorter passages Rowe may simply have over-
looked.

So much for *Hamlet*, but what of the other plays? It was
long ago remarked that in *Romeo and Juliet* Rowe printed
a prologue that is only found in the quarto editions. As,
however, he printed this prologue, not at the beginning of
the play, where the quartos have it, but at the end, it has
been argued that the quarto must have only come to his
knowledge while the play was actually being printed.

So far as I have observed, there are no other clear proofs
of Rowe having used any of the early quartos;[4] but there
is one insertion of his which does ultimately come from a
quarto, though not from a genuine Shakespearian one. In
the fourth act of *Macbeth*, the scene of the witches' cavern,
there occurs in the folios—there is no old quarto text of this
play—a stage direction '*Musicke and a Song. Blacke Spirits,
&c.*', the song itself not being given: Rowe here inserts the
following song:

> Black Spirits and White,
>   Blue Spirits and Gray,
> Mingle, mingle, mingle,
>   You that mingle may,

having in all probability taken it, with the trifling substitution of blue spirits for red ones, from Davenant's adaptation

of *Macbeth*, first printed in 1674, Davenant himself having taken the song, with other matter, from Middleton's play of *The Witch*, a play the relation of which to *Macbeth* is still an unsettled problem. As, however, Rowe did not give the words of another song, 'Come away, come away', which is similarly indicated by the folio and given in full by Davenant from *The Witch*, we may, I think, reasonably suppose, not that Rowe had taken the trouble to collate Davenant's version with the folio text, but that he had seen the play acted—or possibly read it—and chanced to remember the little song which he inserted. It is perhaps worth mentioning that this 'Black Spirits and White' song remained part of the text of *Macbeth* through all the editions from Rowe's to that of Capell, who first threw it out.

There seems therefore to have been little justification for Rowe's claim to have consulted all the available editions of Shakespeare in the preparation of his text. It is in fact little more—at least with the exception of *Hamlet*—than a revision of the Fourth Folio. At the same time it is only fair to admit that it is on the whole a careful and, for its date and purpose, an intelligent revision. Apart from the correction of grammatical errors Rowe was a conservative editor and seldom tampered with anything that made sense, or tried to introduce gratuitous improvements without a reasonable ground for supposing the extant text to be wrong, though there is one instance of this sufficiently curious to seem worth a mention. It occurs in *Troilus and Cressida* (II. ii. 166–7), where Hector uses the phrase

> Unlike young men, whom Aristotle thought
> Unfit to hear moral philosophy.

Doubtless on the ground that Hector, being in date some 800 years antecedent to Aristotle, could not very well quote him, Rowe tried to save Shakespeare's reputation for historical knowledge by substituting for the name 'Aristotle' the words 'graver sages'. Curiously enough, Theobald later, not realizing that the reading originated with Rowe, attacked Pope for having introduced it.

But more important perhaps than Rowe's somewhat haphazard revision of the text itself was the work which he did in introducing uniformity into the designation of the characters, in adding lists of Dramatis Personae where these were wanting in the folios, in correcting the stage directions, especially the entrances and exits, and, in the later plays, in dividing the text into scenes and adding the localities of each; all of which improvements add greatly to the convenience of the reader. To read Shakespeare in Rowe's edition must have been a very different thing from reading him in the Fourth Folio, and we ought not, I think, to refuse to recognize that in all probability it was to Rowe and his publisher Tonson that the beginning of the world-wide recognition of Shakespeare was due.

First, as regards the characters. It is well known that in the early texts of many of the plays characters appear under different names in different parts of the play. Thus in the *Comedy of Errors* the father of the brothers Antipholus is in the text named Aegeon, but in none of the stage directions. nor in the speakers' names, does 'Aegeon' appear. Instead he is variously described as 'Merchant of Syracuse', 'Merchant', 'Merchant Father', and simply 'Father'. This does not, I think, imply that the stage directions and speakers' names were added by some 'editor' but merely that the author, to whom Aegeon was a clear-cut and distinct personality, was in each case thinking of the function which at the moment he performed in the action of the play, and instinctively, and naturally, gave him the designation which this function called for. To the reader, however, these changes are disconcerting, and we may be thankful to Rowe that in his edition 'Aegeon' is 'Aegeon' wherever he appears, and that in the same play the person who is in the folios sometimes 'Angelo' and sometimes 'Goldsmith' has become 'Angelo' throughout.

Similarly in *Love's Labour's Lost*, Ferdinand, King of Navarre, is in the stage directions of the early editions sometimes 'Ferdinand', sometimes 'Navarre', and sometimes

'King'. Rowe calls him 'King' throughout. In *A Midsummer Night's Dream*, Puck appears in headings and stage directions sometimes as 'Robin' or 'Robin Goodfellow' and sometimes as 'Puck'. Rowe has in all cases 'Puck', and is indeed responsible for the introduction of Puck as a proper name. Shakespeare would, I think, have said that his name was 'Robin', or 'Robin the Puck', 'Puck' being really a common noun equivalent to goblin or sprite. In the text he is referred to as 'sweet puck', 'my gentle puck', 'gentle puck', 'an honest puck', 'the puck'—only the first of these suggesting that 'puck' is in any way a personal name.

It may have been his work in regularizing the names of the characters that led Rowe to see the need for a list of Dramatis Personae before each play: indeed he could hardly do the one thing without constructing the other. None of the early quartos has such a list, and only seven plays in the folios. Rowe constructed lists for all the other plays and amplified the existing ones. These have formed the basis of the lists of Dramatis Personae of all later editions, though they have been to some extent modified.

As regards the stage directions it need only be said that Rowe seems to have gone through the plays with some care in order to make sure that the entrances and exits of the characters were correctly indicated. He did not otherwise add much, though he occasionally varied the wording.[5] It is perhaps to be regretted that Rowe did not do more for the stage directions, for had he done this we might well have been able to learn from them something as to the traditional business surviving to his day in those plays that still held the stage. There are many points on which enlightenment would be welcome.

Whether Shakespeare had in writing his plays any idea in his mind of a division into five acts is an unsettled question. Clearly, however, the manuscripts from which the plays were printed were not by any means all divided. Thus none of the quartos printed before the folio of 1623 has any act divisions, with the exception of *Othello*. None of these quartos is divided into scenes.[6]

In the First Folio six plays are printed without divisions of any kind; one, *Hamlet*, is divided as far as the second act, the rest of the play being undivided; eleven plays are divided into acts alone, the remaining eighteen into acts and scenes. There is thus every possible variety. As, moreover, the plays fully divided in the folio include some which were printed from undivided quartos, it seems reasonable to suppose that the division was in all cases the work of the compilers of the folio and to attribute the imperfect way in which it is carried out to their carelessness.

Now when Rowe began his work it does not seem to have occurred to him that this point was of importance, for he left the Comedies as he found them, with the exception of the *Merchant of Venice* which he divided into scenes partially corresponding to those of an adaptation of the play by George Granville published in 1701 as *The Jew of Venice*. In the Histories he merely readjusted the act division in the first part of *Henry VI* and divided the third part, previously undivided, into acts, splitting one act into scenes. When, however, he came to *Troilus and Cressida*, the first of the Tragedies, he began to take the matter more seriously, and from this point onwards he introduced scene division into all the plays where this did not already exist, though his divisions are occasionally, as in *Coriolanus*, somewhat erratic. In general he divided into fewer scenes than the modern editors, even in one case, *King Lear*, making fewer divisions than the folio, eighteen instead of twenty-three: modern editions generally have twenty-six.[7]

Thus although Rowe deserves credit for beginning to tidy up the text of Shakespeare in the matter of act and scene division, he did not carry out his task with any completeness, and the same thing may be said of his other notable addition, that of the localities of the action.

We need not enter into the vexed question of whether indications of locality are desirable in an edition of

Shakespeare, or whether, as some hold, Shakespeare gives us in the actual dialogue all that we need know, and when no particular locality is mentioned the scene is not intended to be precisely localized. We are to imagine two or three people meeting and talking and to concentrate our attention upon what they say to one another without troubling to inquire whether they are in the street or in a house or in the open country or where, which is a matter of not the least consequence. There is, I think, something to be said for this view, but, be this as it may, it is undoubtedly true that many readers find it far easier to appreciate dialogue if they can place the characters somewhere. Without a locality they cannot *see* them, and if they are not *seen* their conversation carries no conviction. It is indeed likely to produce as little impression and to be as tedious to follow as many of us find a broadcast of a play which we have not previously seen on the stage. No doubt then the addition of localities begun by Rowe assisted in the popularity of Shakespeare's plays by making them more generally readable.

There are no indications of locality at all in the quartos and only two general ones in the folios, where the scene of *The Tempest* is said to be 'an vn-inhabited Island' and that of *Measure for Measure* 'Vienna'. Rowe added general localities for other plays and, in a few of the Comedies and in all the Tragedies, the localities of the particular scenes. He did not, however, as modern editors do, indicate the place of action at the head of every scene, but only where he regarded it as changing. Thus even at the beginning of an act no locality is given if it is supposed to be the same as that of the last scene of the previous act—a system which is a little confusing until one understands it. Rowe's indications of locality have been subjected to a good deal of improvement by later editors, but he did at least show others what had to be done.

What has been regarded as the second edition[7]* of Rowe's Shakespeare appeared in 1714 in nine duodecimo volumes.

It is a little difficult to know what to make of this. On the one hand it does not, as one would expect a revised edition to do, carry out in the earlier volumes those improvements in scene division and localization which Rowe had only begun to introduce in the later volumes of his first edition. On the other hand the text, while not without errors of its own, corrects many misprints of the edition of 1709, apparently from the Fourth, or, at least in one case, from an earlier folio.[8] It is, I think, doubtful whether Rowe had much to do with this edition. It may, indeed, have been entirely the work of a certain 'Mr. Hughes'—presumably John Hughes, the poet and editor of Spenser—to whom Tonson paid £28 7s. 0d. in connexion with it.

Rowe's editions are the last in which Shakespeare is treated as a contemporary, or at any rate recent, writer, who can be understood without more elucidation than can be afforded by simply modernizing the spellings. Although the next edition, that of Pope, appeared only sixteen years later than Rowe's first edition or eleven years later than his so-called second, Shakespeare seems by that time to have become an old author requiring explanation and commentary for the average educated person. On 2 August 1721 the Bishop of Rochester, Francis Atterbury, who could hardly be called unlearned, wrote to Pope:

I have found time to read some parts of Shakespeare, which I was least acquainted with. I protest to you in a hundred places I cannot construe him: I do not understand him. The hardest part of Chaucer is more intelligible to me than some of those scenes, not merely through the faults of the edition, but the obscurity of the writer, for obscure he is, and a little (not a little) inclined now and then to bombast, whatever apology you may have contrived on that head for him. There are allusions in him to an hundred things, of which I knew nothing and can guess nothing. And yet without some competent knowledge of those matters there is no understanding him. I protest Æschylus does not want a comment to me more than he does.[9]

It was less than a century since the publication of the First Folio, but Shakespeare had become unintelligible to a man who was by no means ignorant of English literature, and one to whom Milton was a favourite poet. It is rather remarkable when we remember that a longer period separates us now from the work of Scott, of Byron, and of Jane Austen, which, so far as intelligibility is concerned, might also be contemporary, than separated Atterbury from that of Shakespeare.

Unfortunately there seems to be little record of the inception of Pope's edition of Shakespeare, and we may conclude that it arose simply out of a business offer of Tonson's, to whom it might reasonably seem that the foremost poet and critic of the day was the best possible man to edit our foremost dramatist. Work on the book seems to have begun soon after the completion of Pope's translation of the *Iliad*, the final volume of which was issued in May 1720, and by 1723 the text of five out of the six volumes of the Shakespeare—if not of the whole six—was printed, though the edition was not actually published until March 1725, owing apparently to Pope's delay over his Preface.

Before we consider what Pope actually did for the text of Shakespeare, let us get rid of one or two accessory matters in which he carried out improvements begun by Rowe. He kept Rowe's lists of Dramatis Personae almost unchanged, but he improved greatly upon his indications of locality, giving these carefully throughout all the plays, instead of only in the later ones as Rowe had done. He also divided all the plays fully into scenes, following, though not always very strictly, the Italian and French custom of marking a new scene whenever a character of importance enters or leaves the stage. Pope's disposition of the scenes was followed by Hanmer and with certain modifications by Warburton and Johnson. It means, of course, a far larger number of scenes than are found in modern editions. *King Lear*, which as we saw had eighteen scenes in Rowe's edition and twenty-six in most modern ones, has in Pope's no less than sixty.

Rowe, basing his text upon the Fourth Folio, had fol-

lowed the order of the plays in that edition, and had included in his last volume, with *Anthony and Cleopatra* and
Cymbeline, *Pericles* and the six pseudo-Shakespearian plays
which had been first added in the Third Folio. Pope rejected all seven plays as undoubtedly spurious, and for some
reason which he does not explain rearranged the whole in
a new order, grouping them as Comedies; Historical Plays,
in which he includes *King Lear*; 'Tragedies from History',
including most of the classical plays and *Macbeth*; and
'Tragedies from Fable', including *Troilus and Cressida*, *Cymbeline*, *Romeo and Juliet*, *Hamlet*, and *Othello*. The result was,
it is true, six volumes of fairly equal bulk, but if there is any
other justification for the arrangement, it is not easy to dis-
cover this.

But we must pass to the text itself. Pope evidently took
his work seriously. He had tried to enlist the aid of Atterbury, and there are indications that he welcomed corrections and suggestions from others. He also did his best to
collect, or at least obtain access to, as many of the early
editions of the plays as possible, especially all quartos prior
to 1616, the year of Shakespeare's death, for he regarded
those published after that date as without authority.[10] At the
end of his edition he gives a list of quartos used by him, from
which we see that he had, or was aware of, at least one
quarto edition of every play of which quartos are known to
exist, except of *Much Ado about Nothing*, though he had *first*
quartos of only six, namely, *Romeo and Juliet*, of which he had
both the first imperfect one and the first good one, *Love's
Labour's Lost*, *The Merchant of Venice*, the second part of
Henry IV, *Henry V*, and *Troilus and Cressida* (both issues).
He seems to have had a complete set of the 1619 quartos.
He had also a copy of the First Folio, and apparently of the
Second.

Apart from the introduction of new readings either from
other texts or conjectural emendations of obscure passages,
to which I will refer later, the work done by Pope on the
text of Rowe, which he used as the basis of his edition,

consists mainly in further modernizing the spelling, in improving the punctuation, which, in spite of Theobald's strictures, is in Pope's edition on the whole very careful, in redividing the lines where the metre requires this, and in regularizing the printing of the text according as it was prose or verse.

Such changes as these would be generally accepted as quite legitimate in a modern-spelling edition. But Pope went farther in his desire to improve the text of Shakespeare, and it is these further emendations which have caused him to be looked on as an injudicious meddler.

He not only went beyond Rowe in his substitutions of more modern for older usages, printing, for example, 'if' for 'and' or 'an' in such phrases as 'and it were', but made a number of verbal changes for the sake of greater metrical regularity. To give a couple of examples, in the *Two Gentlemen of Verona* he reads 'Lady, good day' for 'Gentlewoman, good day' because the latter phrase is metrically awkward at the beginning of a line, and in *Hamlet* he replaces 'Dared to the combat' by 'Dared to the fight' for a similar reason. But this was not all, for he made a certain number of alterations in the text for which he could not even plead the exigencies of metre as an excuse. One may perhaps be permitted to suspect that in making these changes Pope was not thinking solely of Shakespeare. The author whom he edited and professed to admire might be permitted to be at times too bombastic, at others too flat, to mix his metaphors, or to indulge in other stylistic offences, for he belonged to a less cultured age; but there seem to have been certain things which a literary man of Pope's eminence simply could not let him do, such as to refer to 'hats' in a classical play. It seems odd, in view of the many anachronisms that Pope allowed to pass, even allowing Caesar to pluck open his doublet, that he should so much have objected to Coriolanus waving his hat. But the fact remains that finding 'hat' four times in the plays on classical subjects, twice in *Coriolanus*, once in *Timon of*

Athens, and once in *Julius Caesar*, Pope in the first three cases altered 'hat' to 'cap'. In the fourth there was a difficulty; the phrase was 'Their hats are pluck'd about their ears', and I suppose that he did not quite see how one could do this with a cap. Still 'hat' could not be allowed to stand, so he cut the word out and substituted a dash.

So much for those of Pope's alterations which must be regarded rather as attempts to improve Shakespeare than to recover what he actually wrote. We come now to the more important question of his attempts to restore the text by the use of the earlier editions. And here we must remember, that though Rowe had professed to give the true readings from the several editions and to supply the omissions of the later texts, his actual performance in this respect was very slight. Pope with all his shortcomings was the first editor of Shakespeare to make a genuine attempt to collect all the available material and to use it for the construction of what he regarded as the best possible text, and for this I think we may be grateful to him.

Unfortunately, however, having got his material together, Pope used it in an entirely wrong fashion, owing to his failure to appreciate a very elementary point in textual criticism. In this he was not alone, for failure to appreciate the point in question seems to have been common to all Pope's immediate successors, with the single exception of Johnson; and indeed I am not sure that even now, in spite of the stress which has been laid upon it in recent years by Dr. Pollard and others, it is as well understood as it should be. It is not that there is anything at all abstruse in it; it is just one of those simple and obvious things that we tend most easily to overlook because for generations everybody else has been doing the same. The matter is so important that I must be pardoned for a short digression.

All the early editors of Shakespeare, with the exception of Johnson, who though I think he saw the truth did not altogether follow it, make it perfectly clear either by their prefaces or by their text, or by both, that they considered

that the way to form a good text of Shakespeare was by
comparing as many as possible of the early editions and
taking from them the best readings. How they were to
select the 'best', though a matter, one would think, of some
importance, is not usually discussed. Now the least consideration of the material available to them for selection
would have shown them that if they aimed, as they
evidently did, at reconstructing as nearly as possible the
text as Shakespeare wrote it, such a method was absurd.
They knew, as well as we do, that each edition of a book
after the first is normally printed from an earlier edition and
not from a fresh manuscript, and that in almost every case
it is perfectly easy to make out the line of descent of any
series of printed texts. If they had thought for a moment,
they would have seen that no reading which appears in a
later text, but not in the one from which that later text was
printed, can possibly have any authority except on the
extremely unlikely assumption that the text used as copy
had, before being so used, been corrected from a manuscript; a state of affairs which, if it exists, will almost always
show itself unmistakably. The truth is, of course, that new
readings of authority can never be obtained by comparing
texts in the same line of descent, where the earliest must
obviously be the most authoritative, but only by comparing
texts in different lines of descent.

The explanation of their failure to appreciate so obvious
a fact is that the eighteenth-century editors of Shakespeare
had, of course, received a classical education, and the
textual criticism to which they were accustomed was the
criticism of classical texts. Now in the great majority of cases
the available sources of classical texts are manuscripts each
of which represents the end of a line of descent; only in rare
cases does it occur that a manuscript and one of its direct
ancestors have both survived, and when this *does* occur the
descendant would in practice be ignored. Now when we
have to deal with manuscripts each of which may represent the end of a separate line of descent, none being

demonstrably the ancestor of any other, and supposing that, as is frequently the case, we have insufficient evidence to enable us to work out their relationships with certainty, we are bound to assume that any particular reading in *any* manuscript, even if it differs from the reading of every other manuscript, *may* be correct, for it may have come down, through the lost ancestors of that manuscript alone, from the author's original copy.[11] And this may evidently be the case even if the manuscript containing the reading under consideration is in general a particularly bad one. The existence, therefore, of several manifest errors in a passage constitutes no argument that other words in the passage, which seem to be correct, are wrong. Clearly then if we are dealing with manuscripts it may be a quite reasonable and indeed necessary proceeding to collate all that are available and consider the claim of every separate reading to represent the original words of the author.

It appears to me that it simply never occurred to men like Pope, Theobald, and Capell that the Shakespeare quartos were not in the same position with respect to the author's original text as the classical manuscripts were, in that they did not represent ends of separate lines of descent from it, but in most cases successive members of a single line. If they had reflected they would have seen that if we want Shakespeare's original text the only place where we have any chance of finding it is in a quarto or folio which is at the head of a line of descent, and that if descendants of such a quarto or folio have different readings from their ancestor, those readings must be either accidental corruptions or deliberate alterations by compositors or proof-readers, and can in no case have an authority superior to, or even as great as, the readings of the text from which they differ.

Pope's list of quartos collected by him contains twenty-nine items, excluding the non-Shakespearian *Taming of A Shrew*, and while it would be hazardous to say that he did actually make use of all of them, it is evident that he used the majority. Of those in which the most important differences exist between the folio and quarto texts, namely, *Hamlet, Lear,* and *Romeo and Juliet,* he certainly made very considerable use. In *Hamlet,* as we have seen, Rowe had restored some 131 lines out of the 231 omitted by the folios: Pope restored a further 36. In *Lear,* where the folios had omitted about 284, none of which had been inserted by Rowe in his text, Pope restored 142, exactly half. In the case of *Romeo and Juliet* Pope's use of the first quarto though extensive was somewhat different, for he used it mainly as an excuse for omitting what he calls 'a great number of the mean conceits and ribaldries' that are found in the later texts.

It is difficult to make out exactly how Pope used the quartos and the First Folio. Some have written as though he only consulted them when he found Rowe's text unsatisfactory, and made no attempt to collate them throughout, and in certain cases he seems undoubtedly to have worked in this way. In other cases, however, we find him inserting readings from the earlier editions when there was nothing at all in Rowe's text to suggest that this was wrong. The only possible conclusion is that he had no consistent practice in the matter. Probably he collated those plays, or those passages of plays, which interested him, *throughout,* and for the rest merely consulted the early texts when it seemed to him that the reading before him was unsatisfactory.

As a kind of substitute for detailed criticism Pope had devised a system of printing in smaller type at the foot of the page those passages which in his view were of doubtful authenticity, and this peculiarity of his edition was one of the features for which it was attacked. As a matter of fact, however, several of the passages which he regarded as interpolations, notably the vision in the fifth act of *Cymbeline,* have been rejected by many other critics, and the total amount of matter 'degraded', as he calls it, in his edition, some 1,560 lines, about one and half per cent. of the whole number of lines in the plays, is much less than has been rejected by many more recent writers.

But we must leave Pope, whose edition may be described as the work of a brilliant amateur, a real lover of Shakespeare as he saw him, but one incapable of the long-continued drudgery which was necessary to the accomplishment of the task which he had undertaken, and with no clearer understanding of the problem before him than had others of his time; and come to the man who in many ways was the true founder of modern Shakespearian scholarship, Lewis Theobald, or 'Tebold' or 'Tibbald' as the name seems to have been variously pronounced.

Theobald has come down to us with the reputation of a brilliant emender, on the strength of a few really fine conjectures, of which the best known, Mistress Quickly's words about the dying Falstaff in *Henry V* 'a' babbled of green fields' was, as he fully admits, suggested to him by a marginal correction made by 'a gentleman sometime deceased', who in an edition in Theobald's possession, had emended 'a Table of greene fields' of the Folios, to 'a' talked of green fields'. The truth is, however, that Theobald's far more important claim to recognition is that of having been the first to point out the value of comparing other passages of Shakespeare with those which it is sought to emend—as he himself puts it—'every author is best expounded and explain'd in *One* Place, by his own Usage and Manner of Expression in *Others*'.[12] In his *Shakespeare Restored* and his edition of the plays he constantly supports his emendations by parallel passages, a method which has, of course, been followed by every commentator upon Shakespeare since his day.

Just a year after the publication of Pope's edition of Shakespeare, Theobald issued an attack upon it under the singularly offensive title *Shakespeare restored: or, a Specimen of the Many Errors, as well Committed, as Unamended, by Mr. Pope in his Late Edition of this Poet. Designed not only to correct the said Edition, but to restore the True Reading of Shakespeare in all the Editions ever yet publish'd.* Though the fact does not appear on the title-page, the book is mainly concerned with

Hamlet, to which play 132 out of its 194 pages are devoted, the remaining 62 containing notes on the other plays. The 'corrections' proposed by Theobald in the text of *Hamlet* are about 106, of which 22 are either corrections of obvious misprints in Pope's edition or improvements in his punctuation. Of the remainder, 51 are readings from other editions than those followed by Pope, and it is interesting to notice that 45 of them—all but 6—have been adopted by such a conservative text as the Aldis Wright 'Cambridge' edition. On the other hand, of 33 conjectures of Theobald's, *not* taken from other texts, only three have been adopted by modern editors, of which only one is of importance, the famous 'sanctified and pious bawds' for the 'bonds' of the quartos and folios. Clearly so far as *Hamlet* is concerned the influence of Theobald was far more in the number of almost certainly correct readings which he recovered from the earlier editions than in his own conjectural emendations.

At the date of *Shakespeare Restored* Theobald had already acquired a few quarto editions of the plays, including the 1600 quarto of *Much Ado*, which Pope had not seen, and he evidently continued with great zeal to collect others, being probably still further stimulated by the contemptuous treatment accorded to his book in Pope's second edition of Shakespeare, 1728, where Pope stated that he had taken from Theobald's work as many of the proposed emendations 'as are judg'd of any the least advantage to the poet; the whole amounting to about *twenty-five* words'. By the date of his own edition of 1733 he had obtained, or borrowed, 38 quartos, against the 29 listed by Pope,[13] the new ones including first quartos of *Merry Wives*, *Midsummer Night's Dream*, *Much Ado*, and *Richard III*, though he had no *first* quarto of *Love's Labour's Lost* and none at all of *Troilus and Cressida*.

It seems to be customary among editors of English classics to use as the basis of their own edition that particular earlier one which in their preface they most vehemently condemn; and Theobald followed the custom by using Pope's. This, no doubt, rather than intentional copying, accounts for a good deal of similarity between the two editions in such minor points as stage directions and indications of locality, in which Theobald generally follows the wording of Pope, though he sometimes amplifies it. He also to a certain extent retained Pope's arrangement of the plays, though not his grouping.

When we come to the text itself we find a state of affairs which seems to render it doubtful whether Theobald was really the meticulously careful collator that many have supposed him to be. It is true, of course, that if we compare almost any passage of Theobald's text with Pope's or Rowe's, we find that Theobald has adopted a number of readings from early editions and that the majority of these have been accepted by later editors. Thus in a couple of scenes taken at random from *A Midsummer Night's Dream* and *Julius Caesar* and amounting together to a little more than 500 lines, I find that Theobald introduced no less than fourteen definite improvements of reading which have become part of the accepted text of Shakespeare.[14]

But on the other hand we find, especially in the plays generally regarded as less important, a large number of cases in which Theobald followed Pope in inferior readings although better ones were available in the editions which he professed to have collated. The only possible conclusion seems to be that he used the early editions much as Pope had done, consulting them whenever it struck him that there was anything suspicious in the text before him; but only occasionally, in plays which especially interested him, collating them throughout. At the same time he was evidently more careful or less easily satisfied than Pope, and the total amount of work which he put into his text must have been far greater, while he obviously had a much better knowledge of the English of Shakespeare's time. But it is important to observe that Theobald's text, in spite of its many improvements upon Pope's, was still a text constructed on what we now realize to be a fundamentally wrong principle. It is a text based ultimately, by way of

Pope and Rowe, on the Fourth Folio, *corrected* by earlier editions; that is, a text based on the worst of the pre-Rowe texts and not, as it should have been, on the best of them. The result is that in a host of passages, when the reading of the Fourth Folio, though differing from earlier editions, gives a possible sense, it is this that Theobald followed. It is curious to observe how the modernized texts of Shakespeare have with the progress of time gradually approached closer and closer to the readings of the best of the early texts, but always, until quite recently, by the process of gradually correcting bad texts by the elimination of a larger and larger proportion of their errors, and never by what would seem the much simpler and more obvious method of starting with the good ones and basing the text on these.

But more perhaps than the improvement of the text itself, the feature of Theobald's edition which gives it a place of the first importance in the history of Shakespearian scholarship is his footnotes, which may be said to have initiated the critical study of Shakespeare's language. Pope had for the most part contented himself with merely giving variant readings, without discussion or explanation of any kind. Theobald, on the other hand, comments, sometimes at great length, on the cruxes, giving parallels both from Shakespeare himself and from other authors—he tells us that he had read above 800 English plays for the purpose of his edition: he undoubtedly made much use of his reading and his comments are to the point.

A second edition of Theobald's Shakespeare appeared in 1740, seven years after the first. This is in a smaller size and was intended as a cheap edition. It contains a number of additional emendations in the text, but these are mostly conjectural, and there seems no evidence of the collation of editions not previously used or of the fresh collation of those already collated. The list of quartos printed at the end is identical with that in Theobald's first edition, which is rather strange, as one would have expected so ardent a collector to acquire in those happy days at least *one* early quarto of Shakespeare in seven years.

Little time need be spent over the next edition of Shakespeare, the one prepared by Sir Thomas Hanmer and issued at Oxford in 1743-4 in six spaciously printed volumes. Hanmer seems to have known little and cared less about such matters as early editions or the language of Shakespeare's time, and attempted to reform the text by the light of nature alone, with the result that though his conjectural emendations are sometimes ingenious and seem at first sight attractive, the work as a whole can hardly be regarded as a serious contribution to Shakespearian scholarship.[15]

Nor need I say much about the edition of William Warburton, afterwards Bishop of Gloucester, which was issued in 1747. Warburton was a man of very wide reading and interests, though apparently no great scholar, and had helped Theobald, and, it would seem, also Hanmer, with notes for their editions. He had later quarrelled with both these scholars and determined to bring out an edition of his own. The result may be described as a compound of Theobald's text, from which Warburton's edition was printed, with Pope's scene-numbering and with notes mainly of Warburton's own.[16]

In 1745 Samuel Johnson had published certain *Miscellaneous Observations on the Tragedy of Macbeth*, as a specimen of a projected edition of Shakespeare, and in 1765, twenty years later, the edition appeared. Johnson's Shakespeare is very far from being a satisfactory piece of work; indeed it is imperfect in almost every possible way, but even so it represents a great advance on the editions of Hanmer and Warburton. Its preface alone would render it notable, not only because this is a piece of perfectly efficient writing which expresses with complete clearness and certainty exactly what the writer meant to say, without self-adulation and without unnecessary depreciation of his predecessors, but even more because in it we find the first hint of a rational study of Shakespeare's text. Johnson alone of all the early editors seems to have seen clearly the principles on which textual criticism of printed books must be based. Thus in reference to Theobald he writes:

> In his enumeration of editions, he mentions the two first folios as of high, and the third folio as of middle authority; but the truth is, that the first is equivalent to all others, and that the rest only deviate from it by the printer's negligence. Whoever has any of the folios has all, excepting those diversities which mere reiteration of editions will produce. I collated them all at the beginning, but afterwards used only the first.

We should now, perhaps, to the printer's negligence have added the proof-reader's guesses as a possible cause of the deviations in the later folios, but in other respects Johnson exactly expresses the views held to-day. If only some editors who followed him had pondered over the significance of his words, how much trouble they might have saved themselves and of how many superfluous footnotes would editions of Shakespeare have been relieved.

Johnson made use, as he says, of the First Folio, but he admits that he had been able to procure few of the quartos —he seems to have had access to about seventeen, but only two of these belonged to first editions, and I have found little or no evidence of any minute collation even of those that were known to him. He printed from the text of Warburton, and his edition contains misprints taken over by Warburton from Theobald's second edition. Indeed Johnson's text shows little advance on that of his predecessors, the merit of his edition, apart from the preface, being largely in the illuminating common sense of his notes, and especially of the critical judgements which follow each play.

The last edition to which I propose to refer is that of Edward Capell, which appeared in ten volumes in the year 1768, and I have thought that this edition might conveniently end the series, not because I share the opinion which sees in Capell 'the father of all legitimate commentary on Shakespeare', but because it seems to me that his work represents the climax of the selective type of textual

criticism. Capell seems to have been greatly impressed by
the irresponsibility of Hanmer's treatment of the text in his
edition of 1744, and at once began to collect every edition
of Shakespeare, new and old, that he could procure, with
the result that in a few years he had copies of all the quartos
which had been previously recorded except six, and a
further twelve which up to that time were unknown. He
had thus the largest collection of Shakespeare material that
had ever been assembled, and it is a thing for which all
Cambridge men and indeed all Shakespearians owe him
very lively gratitude that at his death instead of allowing
this collection to be dispersed, he left it to Trinity College
and thus incidentally much facilitated the work of the
Cambridge editors of 1863–6. It may be worth while to
note that Capell had, or knew of, fifty-nine quartos (including those of the *Contention of York and Lancaster*) and
that the total now known (of those falling within the period
with which he concerned himself) amounts to no more than
sixty-nine. Of the ten additional ones three differ merely
in the title-pages from those previously known, so that
actually only seven new editions of Shakespearian quartos
have come to light since his day.[17]

Unfortunately having got together this magnificent
collection of material for editing Shakespeare, Capell did
not know, any better than his predecessors, how to use it.
That he was perfectly capable of working out the relationship of the texts seems obvious from remarks in his preface
concerning modern editions. He saw quite clearly that
editions tend to degenerate with each reprint, but he seems
never to have drawn the inference that Johnson did, that
readings in a late text which differed from those of an
earlier one from which it had itself been printed could not
possibly be of any authority. He is very clear on the point
that though one should base a new edition on whatever
text seems to one best, one should look into the other
editions and select from thence whatever improves the
Author; 'that they do improve him was with the editor an

argument in their favour; and a presumption of genuineness for what is thus selected, whether additions, or differences of any other nature'. Capell's preface is perhaps, in spite of what Johnson called its 'gabble', the clearest exposition of the selective theory of editing—the idea that if an editor likes a reading, that reading is (*a*) good, and (*b*) attributable to Shakespeare.

Capell's edition suffered greatly by being almost entirely without notes or various readings, and having merely a general explanation of how he had constructed his text. He seems to have intended to follow it at once by a series of volumes of notes in which all would be explained—the sources of the emendations adopted and his reasons for adopting them—but it was six years before the first volume appeared and the whole was not issued until 1783, two years after his death, a fact which no doubt told strongly against the acceptance of the edition by his contemporaries.

In spite, however, of this absence of notes, Capell's edition has great merits. He was a careful and thorough collator and seems to have taken infinite pains with his work, and he seems, unlike every editor before him, to have had his text set up from a fresh transcript of his own, instead of from the edition of one of his predecessors, a method which enabled him to avoid an immense number of accumulated corruptions which had hitherto passed unnoticed. He took great care also with subsidiary matters, such as stage directions, in which he is perhaps a little over-elaborate, the localization of scenes, and scene division. In several cases his disposition of the scenes has been accepted by all later editors.

Capell's is probably the best of the eclectic texts of Shakespeare, though it was by no means the last. On the whole, however, Shakespearian study for almost a century after 1768 concerned itself more largely with explanation and commentary than with the improvement of the text, and the attempts at this were, with certain exceptions, somewhat haphazard. Before further progress could be made, minuter study of the conditions of Shakespeare's time, of the theatre, and, above all, of the language was necessary. But the editors at whose work we have been glancing this afternoon did, each in his way, something to make Shakespeare more accessible to the reading public.

To sum up the whole story very briefly. Rowe made the text of Shakespeare more easily readable by a general tidying up of the character-indications, stage directions, and text, and his publisher Tonson assisted by presenting it in a handier form than that of the cumbersome folios. Pope for the first time gave the text serious critical consideration, especially from the point of view of metre, and by attention to the line division, and to the contracted and uncontracted verbal forms, greatly improved the verse in a vast number of passages. He also first made a real attempt to compare the various editions, and freed the text from numerous corruptions. Theobald carried further the use of the early editions, and by readings taken from these and by his own conjectural emendations produced a much better text than that of any previous editor, while by the citation of parallels from Shakespeare himself and from other authors of his time he cleared up many obscurities and brought the idea of textual criticism before the public in a way which none had previously attempted. Of Hanmer and Warburton I need only say that each contributed a few emendations which have been accepted by later critics, and a few useful notes. Johnson realized, as apparently no previous editor had done, the essential difference between the textual criticism of printed texts and that of the classical manuscripts, and in this gave the first suggestion of modern editorial methods. And lastly Capell—I hardly know what to say of Capell, for though he was the most thorough, the most painstaking editor of them all, his edition was somehow a failure, at any rate in its appeal to the public. At the same time, though it was never reprinted, it was greatly used by the editors who came after him, and later texts of Shakespeare owe much to his work. One and all, in their several ways, contributed to the honour of the master to whom they devoted their service, and to all of them we owe our gratitude to-day.

NOTES

1. Apart from the normal modernizations there are in all the folios a certain number of attempts to emend passages which appeared unintelligible, but these were probably mere guesses. There is, further, some evidence that the Second Folio was printed from a copy of the First which contained manuscript corrections (see especially *Richard III*, IV. i. 92–4, and the note of the Cambridge editors), but here again there is nothing to indicate that the corrector had had access to an independent source, while there is much to suggest that he was an incompetent meddler with little knowledge of the language of Shakespeare's time. It is of course impossible to assert that all the changes found in this folio had been made in the copy from which it was printed, but the character of many is consistent with a deliberate attempt to substitute what doubtless appeared at the time easier readings. This had the curious result that in the early eighteenth century the Second Folio was regarded as the best (cf. Theobald's *Shakespeare Restored*, p. 70). Malone later attacked this view and gave a long list of absurd alterations made in this folio through ignorance of Shakespeare's language. He maintained indeed that the corrector of the Second Folio (or perhaps he should have said the corrector of the copy of the First Folio from which it was printed), 'whoever he was, and Mr. Pope, were the two great corrupters of our poet's text' (Preface of 1790; '*Variorum*' 1821, i. 208).

2. In one respect Rowe's text appears to-day more old-fashioned than the Fourth Folio, for he, or his printer, introduced the practice common in his time of capitalizing almost all nouns. Pope's text on the other hand, though printed from Rowe's, has hardly more capitals than a modern edition.

3. The *Evening Post*, May 5, 1722, quoted by Wheatley in *Transactions of the Bibliographical Society*, xiv. 155.

4. There are, however, one or two doubtful cases, the most important of which is perhaps one cited by Dr. Greg in his lecture on *Principles of Emendation in Shakespeare*, p. 45, from *Henry V*, i. ii. 173, where the Fourth Folio has 'To tame and havock'. Rowe in his first edition substitutes for 'tame' (the reading of all the folios) the word 'spoil', which is the reading of the quartos. While at first sight it is natural to conclude that the reading actually comes from a quarto, I feel that this is not altogether certain. It is, I believe, the only case in the play which definitely suggests that a quarto was used, for the remaining instances

of quarto readings found in Rowe's text, such as at I. ii. 197, 243, III. vi. 118, and IV. i. 120, may easily have been his own corrections; while on the other hand there are in the quarto several readings which, if he were aware of them, one would have expected Rowe to adopt. The folio reading 'To tame and havock' was clearly wrong, and 'spoil' was a not unlikely guess. It was, after all, probably a mere guess in the first quarto.

A similar problem arises with respect to *A Midsummer Night's Dream*, III. ii. 260, where for the nonsensical 'thou but' of the later folios Rowe reads 'thou burr' in agreement with the quartos and First Folio. But here again the emendation is one which, in the context, demands no great ingenuity, and it may be merely a happy conjecture.

5. Thus for the odd-looking direction in *3 Henry VI*, II. i, '*Enter one blowing*' Rowe has merely '*Enter a Messenger*', and when, in *Titus Andronicus*, II. i, we have in the folios '*Enter* Chiron *and* Demetrius *braving*', i.e. quarrelling, he omits the word '*braving*'.

6. The text of the first quarto of *Romeo and Juliet* (1597) is in the last third of the play divided by lines of ornament into portions, most, though not all, of which correspond with the accepted scene divisions. I believe, however, that in introducing these ornaments the printer had no intention of marking the scenes, but that his purpose was merely to fill up space and thus help to drive out the matter to the length that it was expected to occupy; the ornaments being naturally inserted at places where there was some interruption in the dialogue. For some unknown reason the type selected for this edition was changed for a smaller one after the first four sheets. A simple calculation shows that the blank lines occurring before and after the stage directions in the later portion of the play, together with the before-mentioned ornaments, occupy almost exactly the amount of space which was saved by the reduction in the size of type. The book is therefore of the same length as it would have been if the larger type had been continued throughout.

7. Including one scene which is not in the folios or Rowe's edition.

8. As an example of the corrections in the 1714 edition of Rowe, I may mention the name of the character in *Hamlet* whom we know as Rosencranz. Rowe's first edition had bestowed upon him the curious name of 'Roseneraus', though the Fourth Folio, which he usually followed, had called him 'Rosincros'. Why Rowe chose to substitute, as he does most carefully everywhere, a form which does not seem to occur in any other text whatsoever, and which upsets the scansion of almost every line in which it occurs, is somewhat of a mystery, unless, possibly, it is explained by the defective printing of the list of Dramatis Personae in one of the 1676 quartos (that with a five-line imprint), where owing to a choked c the name might—at least in the B.M. copy—

be misread as 'Rosinoraus' or 'Rosineraus'. In the edition of 1714 the name is altered throughout, except in the Dramatis Personae, to Rosincrosse, the form though not the spelling given by the Fourth Folio.

A 1714 reading in *2 Henry VI*, i. iii. 46, namely 'Fashion in' where F 1, F 2, F 3 have 'Fashions in' and F 4 and Rowe i have 'Fashion of' (which last reading makes perfectly good sense), seems to indicate that for the duodecimo edition some folio earlier than the fourth was collated.

9. *Works of Alexander Pope*, ed. Elwin and Courthope, ix. 26–7.

10. *Works, v.s.*, viii. 48.

11. In the comparatively rare cases in which the number and character of the surviving manuscripts enable us to construct a satisfactory scheme of descent, we may be able to show that a particular reading cannot be original, e.g. when a manuscript which evidently branched off from the line of descent at a point earlier than the manuscript containing the reading in question agrees with others more closely allied to the latter in presenting a different reading. In such a case the reading under discussion must have arisen at, or after, the branching off of the line terminating in the manuscript which contains it, but not before.

12. *Shakespeare Restored*, p. viii; cf. Preface to his edition of 1733, p. xliii.

13. Including in both cases the imperfect quartos of the second and third parts of *Henry VI* known as *The first part of the Contention of York and Lancaster* and *The true tragedy of Richard Duke of York*. Theobald divided his list of editions into three groups, 'Editions of Authority' (the first two folios and the earlier quartos up to the date of the First Folio), 'Editions of Middle Authority' (the later folios and the quartos after 1623), and 'Editions of No Authority' (the editions of Rowe and Pope); a division which, I believe, has had a very bad effect on Shakespearian criticism as tending to strengthen the idea that the authority of an edition depends upon its date rather than upon its origin. Pope's way of treating all before his own, including Rowe's, as 'the old editions' was a better beginning for a bibliographical inquiry, though not, of course, of much use without the next step of considering the relationship of these editions to one another.

14. A matter which should perhaps be mentioned, as Theobald evidently took much trouble over it, is the punctuation of his edition. His *Shakespeare Restored* showed him to have very definite views on the subject. He revised Pope's punctuation very thoroughly, making it much heavier and in particular greatly increasing the number of commas. Thus in the two scenes mentioned, *A Midsummer Night's Dream*, i. i, and *Julius Caesar*, iii. ii, amounting to 523 lines in all, Theobald inserted no less than 80 commas and replaced 34 of Pope's commas by

semicolons, besides substituting a few colons for semicolons and adding some full stops to Pope's dashes. By modern standards Theobald's punctuation is much too heavy.

15. As instances of Hanmer's more curious emendations may be mentioned his substitution of 'Bythinia' for 'Bohemia' as a locality in *The Winter's Tale*, on account, of course, of the well-known difficulty about the sea-coast, and his ingenious but absurd correction of Costard's phrase for Moth in *Love's Labour's Lost*, III. i. 136, 'my incony Jew' to 'my ink-horn, adieu!' But it would be quite unfair to judge his edition by these two oddities.

16. Much of Warburton's best work on Shakespeare is contained in the notes which he contributed to Theobald's edition. These are for the most part explanatory and critical, but include a few good emendations such as 'the wolf behowls the moon' in *Midsummer Night's Dream*, v. i. 379, an improvement on the 'beholds' of all the early texts which has been universally accepted. The new matter contributed by his own edition is relatively unimportant, though he does seem to have collated certain quartos afresh.

17. In his list of quartos Capell includes an undated *Othello*, which he probably took over from Pope's list, and which appears to be only a shaved copy of the edition of 1622. I have therefore omitted it from the count. Of the 59 quartos listed Capell seems to have possessed 51 and to have seen another 4, leaving only 4 included on the reports of others. Twelve quartos are marked by him as not previously recorded. It may, I think, have been disgust at finding that the list of quartos contributed by Steevens to Johnson's edition of 1765 contained no less than eight out of these twelve that decided Capell to ignore Johnson's edition as completely as he did, though it may have been quite true that a great part of his own edition was already printed when Johnson's appeared (Capell's 'Introduction', p. 19, note).

7* Since this lecture was printed in pamphlet form, I have discovered a hitherto unnoticed edition of Rowe's Shakespeare in six octavo volumes intermediate between the original edition of 1709 and the duodecimo of 1714, which was therefore the third, at least. This intermediate edition, which must henceforth be regarded as the second, is a close, line for line reprint of the first, and, like it, is dated 1709, though it appears to have been printed in the following year (see my letter on the subject in the *Times Literary Supplement* of 8 March 1934, p. 168). The differences of reading between the two editions are comparatively few and for the most part were probably accidental. Nevertheless, a certain number of emendations which have been generally adopted by later editors are found for the first time in the reprint, such as 'Unrip'dst' for 'Unrip'st' in *Richard III*, I. iv. 212, 'walls' for 'walks' in *Julius Caesar*, I. ii. 155, 'tune' for 'time' in *Macbeth*, IV. iii. 235, 'Does't' for 'Dost' in *Othello*, II. iii. 380, and 'King's' for 'Kings' in *Cymbeline*, II. iii. 149. There seems, however, to be no evidence of any general and systematic revision.